WALKING CLOSE TO

RUTLAND WATER

Number Six in the popular series of walking guides

ontents

alked, Written and Drawn by Clive Brown
Clive Brown 2002
2nd Edition 2005 – 2013, 3rd Edition 2014.

lished by Clive Brown
N 978-1-907669-06-4

PLEASE
Take care of the countryside
Your leisure is someone's livelihood

Close gates
Start no fires
Keep away from livestock and animals
Do not stray from marked paths
Take litter home
Do not damage walls, hedgerows or fences
Cross only at stiles or gates
Protect plants, trees and wildlife
Keep dogs on leads
Respect crops, machinery and rural property
Do not contaminate water

Although not essential we recommend good walking boots; during hot weather take something to drink on the way. All walks can easily be negotiated by an averagely fit person. The routes have been recently walked and surveyed, changes can however occur, please follow any signed diversions. Some paths cross fields which are under cultivation. All distances and times are approximate.

The maps give an accurate portrayal of the area, but scale has however been sacrificed in some cases for the sake of clarity and to fit restrictions of page size.

Walking Close To have taken every care in the research and production of this guide but cannot be held responsible for the safety of anyone using them.

During very wet weather, parts of these walks may become impassable through flooding, check before starting out. Stiles and rights of way can get overgrown during the summer; folding secateurs are a useful addition to a walker's rucksack.

Thanks to Angela for help in production of these booklets

Views or comments?
walkingcloseto@yahoo.co.uk

Reproduced from Ordnance Survey Mapping on behalf of The Controller of Her Majesty's Stationery Office.   © Crown Copyright License No. 100037980.

6

Walking Close to
Rutland Water

Jtland, historically England's smallest county, lost 3% of its land area with the
eation of Rutland Water in the mid seventies. Created by the damming of the
Illey of the River Gwash, water is supplied to the reservoir from pumping stations
1 the Nene at Wansford and the Welland close to Stamford. Rutland Water is part
' an Anglian Water network, which includes Grafham Water and Pitsford Water
Ipplying water to the large population in the surrounding area.

has since become a haven for wildlife, particularly wildfowl. The jewel in its
own is the recent return of the osprey to England; although they have experienced
roblems breeding and still have only a precarious hold on their territory.

Jtland Water is also a magnet for water sports of all descriptions, yachts large and
nall, sailboards, speedboats towing water skiers and rowing boats with anglers
owd the lake winter and summer, weekend and weekday.

tarmac and hardcore path runs all the way around the lake, but at close to twenty
iles in length it is more popular with cyclists than walkers. This booklet makes use
' these paths in a series of shorter circular walks.

ie Great Hall is the only surviving part of Oakham Castle (walk no. 8), it houses an
teresting collection of decorative horseshoes, a local custom dictates that any
obleman as well as members of the Royal Family must pay one horseshoe as a toll
1 visiting the town for the first time.

ie Castle Cement factory dominates the eastern end of Rutland's skyline; walk no.
passes close by their extensive quarries.

Jtland County Council has made walking within its boundaries considerably easier
Ith its widespread use of yellow topped marker posts; keep a watchful eye for
ese during your walks.

ie maps give an accurate portrayal of the area, but scale has however been
crificed in some cases for the sake of clarity and to fit restrictions in page size.

e feel that it would be difficult to get lost with the instructions and maps in this
ooklet, but recommend carrying an Ordnance Survey map. All walks are on
kplorer Map No. 234; Landranger Nos. 130 & 141 cover at a smaller scale. Roads,
:ographical features and buildings, not on our map but visible from the walk can
: easily identified.

1 Sounding Bridge

6$^1/_2$ Miles   3 Hours

Park in Manton village, no toilets, pub the 'Horse and Jockey'

1 Cross the stile over the road from the bottom corner of the 'Horse and Jockey' at the north west corner of the village. Walk along the left hand edge of the field t the gate and step over the stile. Go over the A6003 and the stile on the other side Go down the left hand side of this field, through the gate and over the two stiles in the middle of the end fence. Maintain direction over the next field, which may be under cultivation although the track should be visible through the crop; continue across the ridged field to the corner of the wall ahead.

2 Carry on along the bridleway with the wall to the left, across the farm road wit the double concrete tracks. At the next boundary cross the field diagonally to the small clump of conifers, the path should be visible within the crop. Go past the marker post at the hedge gap and follow the right hand side of the field, past the wood, to the pylon.

3 Cross the field to the gap in the hedge, the track should be visible through any crop, keep direction over the next two fields and stile/footbridges. Walk past the end of a copse to a yellow topped marker post and cross the small section of field the hedge corner diagonally slightly left. Follow the hedge for 100yds and go over to the yellow top post in the bottom right corner. Step over the stile, go down the right hand edge of the field, past the pond to a stile, cross, turn left and walk into the village of Brooke.

4 Go past the church and turn back to walk along the other side before bearing left with the road. Continue on the road as it becomes a hardcore bridleway, crosses the River Gwash by a stone bridge and goes uphill past Hillside Croft. Go through the gate, along the right hand side of the field, through another gate and past the pylon.

5 At the gate in the corner bear right along the enclosed bridleway, past Brooke Covert East, the wood on the left, go through the gate and down the left hand edg of the field. Continue through another gate, down this enclosed bridleway and carefully over the railway and the busy A6003 road.

6 Keep direction up the road ahead into the village of Egleton and carry on dowr the path by the side of the road into the car park.

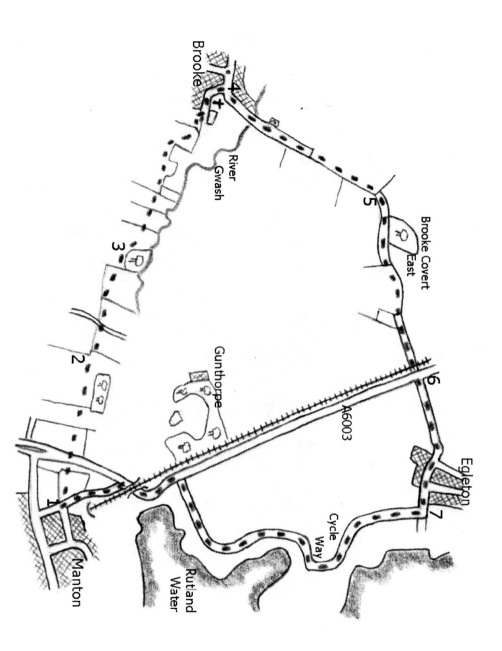

Turn right at the car park down the hardcore cycleway and keep on going as it twists and turns for a mile and a half to the road. Turn left at the road and walk round the corner and under the bridge. Turn sharp left just the other side; go through the gate and up the wide cycleway back to the pub, the village and your vehicle.

2 Lyndon Wood

4 Miles   2 Hours

Park in the visitor centre car park off the Edith Weston to Manton road close to the lake. Charge payable for a permit which also includes entry to the nature reserve and bird hides.

1 Walk away from the car park along the path and cycle track surrounding the lake in an anti-clockwise, easterly direction. Continue for just over a quarter of a mile to the signpost on the right. Turn right through the double wooden gates and the next gates, keep direction uphill to the middle of the field; turn left and walk to the top corner. Go through the gate, cross a rough double track road and a patch of grass; carry on through the gate straight ahead and turn right. Carry on down the right hand edge of the field to the road.

2 Cross this surprisingly busy road carefully and turn left along the road for 200yds; take the signposted bridleway to the right. Maintain direction past the wood through the gate at the bottom. Bear left upslope through the gate on to the road and turn left into Lyndon village. Carry straight on at the crossroads to the signpost on the right at the far end of the village.

3 Turn right, and follow the track with the railings to the right and then left, around the field and past the ha-ha. Turn left at the bottom corner down to the marker post and then right through the narrow belt of trees. Go to the left along the field edge, turn right in the corner and continue to the hardcore farm road. Turn left and follow the road to the right at the next corner and carry on past the plantation to the marker post.

4 Turn right at this junction of paths and maintain direction uphill along the right hand side of the field, all the way to the road. Join the minor road briefly to the left and cross back over the busier road carefully; keep ahead across the cattle grid and carry on down this driveway past the pill box and down the hill to the visitor centre and your vehicle in the car park.

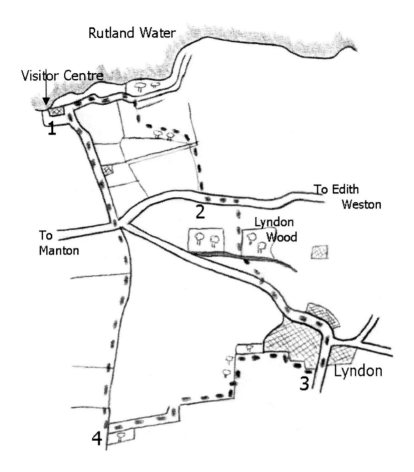

Rutland Water

Visitor Centre

1

To Edith Weston

2

Lyndon Wood

To Manton

H

Lyndon

3

4

The disused quarry in Exton Park, (walk no 6), was the first home of the giant dragline earth mover, Sundew, named after the 1957 Grand National Winner. This machine weighed 1675 tons and had a bucket capacity of 27 tons. It moved by 'walking' on two massive feet. In 1974, after the quarry's closure and a two year planning period the crane went on a thirteen mile, nine week journey, walking all the way to Corby. On the way it crossed a river, a railway line and ten major roads; it worked until 1980 and spent another few years effectively in storage before it was scrapped in 1987. The cab survives as a museum exhibit at the railway museum in Cottesmore.

3 Manton Junction

5$^1/_2$ Miles   2$^1/_2$ Hours

Park in Manton village, no toilets, pub the 'Horse and Jockey'

1 Start from the front of the 'Horse and Jockey', walk uphill to the Manton to Edit
Weston road. Turn right and cross carefully over the deceptively busy A6003 at the
junction, continue along the bridleway opposite. Maintain direction through the
metal gates and cross the field to the yellow topped post.

2 Turn left at the post and walk down the slope to the Fox Covert, go down the
track through the edge of the trees. Continue past the pylon and down the left
hand edge of the next two fields, through the gate and cross the field on a left han
diagonal to the metal gate in the left hand hedge (look for the yellow topped post
on the other side of the gate). This field may be under cultivation but the path
should be visible through any crop. Keep direction across the next field; 40yds from
the hedge fork right, cross the stile/footbridge and go over the corner of the field to
the stile in the left hand end of the hedge (it may be easier to go to the right,
around the edge). Stop over the stile and continue ahead along the field edge, go
straight on as the hedge ends over the farm road to the stile in the top left corner,
turn right along the verge of the A6003 into Preston village.

3 At the crossroads in Preston turn left and carry on down this road for nearly a
mile to the T-junction.

4 Bear right and right again at the junction after 200yds; walk downhill over the
railway bridge to the footpath sign on the left opposite the next junction.

5 Cross the field and then the railway by the yellow topped post, maintain
direction on the other side over the rough stone road and up the slope to the top
right hand corner of the field, which will possibly have a crop in, but the path shoul
be marked. Go into the next field and take a slight right hand diagonal to the
marker post. Walk up the tree lined track into Wing village.

6 At the road turn right then left into Middle Street. Go left along Bottom Street
for 300yds and turn right over the stile at the signpost. Walk down the edge of the
field with the fence to the left, cross the stile on the left and go downhill across the
footbridge over the River Chater.

7 Cross and bear left, go through the hedge and continue to the far corner by the
railway bridge; go under the bridge and turn right up the signposted path next to
the railway. Keep going along this path past Manton railway junction, although it
may not be in sight. The path runs along a tarmac road and then down a short
stretch of enclosed path next to it, re-joining and continuing on tarmac and concre
to the road. Turn left back into Manton and your vehicle.

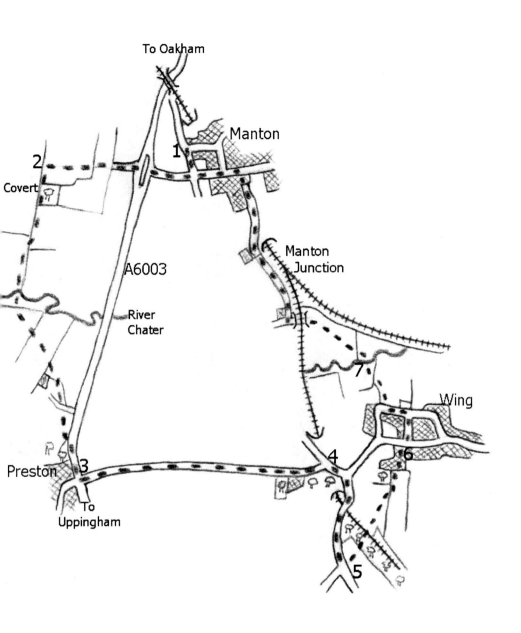

To Oakham

Manton

1

2

Covert

A6003

River
Chater

Manton
Junction

7

Wing

3

Preston

To
Uppingham

4

6

5

4   Lost Village

But don't be too disappointed as there's very little to see!

5 Miles $2^1/_2$ Hours

Park in Manton village, no toilets, pub the 'Horse and Jockey'.

1   Walk down the sloping road to the left of the Horse and Jockey past the sign saying 'No access to Rutland Water'. Go through the gate at the bottom and turn right under the railway bridge and along the road. When the path stops continue along the verge of the A6003 to the bridleway sign.

2   Turn left, cross the railway and bear right, through an entrance into the trees. Follow the obvious track through the wood. Turn right at the exit and keep going around the edge of the field. Go through the gate in the top right hand corner and turn right, bear left along the road with the holly hedge to the left. Continue past the stables and the house through the green gate, along the left hand field edge.

3   Join the double track concrete road ahead. Just past the cattle grid, change sides and walk along left hand edge of the right hand field with the hedge on the left. Keep going along the left hand side of the second field to the top left corner; go through a tree lined gateway and down the right hand side of this field. Bear right at the end through a gateway and down a hedge lined track to a hardcore bridleway.

4   Turn left over the bridge and into the village of Brooke. Walk past the church up the slope and turn left at the green triangle, signposted Uppingham. Continue uphill to the crossroads and turn left, signposted America Lodge.

5   Keep direction along this bridleway when the tarmac stops, cross a cattle grid and walk past a pylon. As the information board states, a large house and a village called Martinsthorpe existed here until the 17th century. Go past the remaining stone building, Old Hall Farm, to the right. Cross the fence and follow the right hand fence to the gate; go through and keep direction along the line of trees to the yellow top post. Continue through the gate and along the bridleway to the road. Cross the A6003 and walk down the road into Manton and your vehicle.

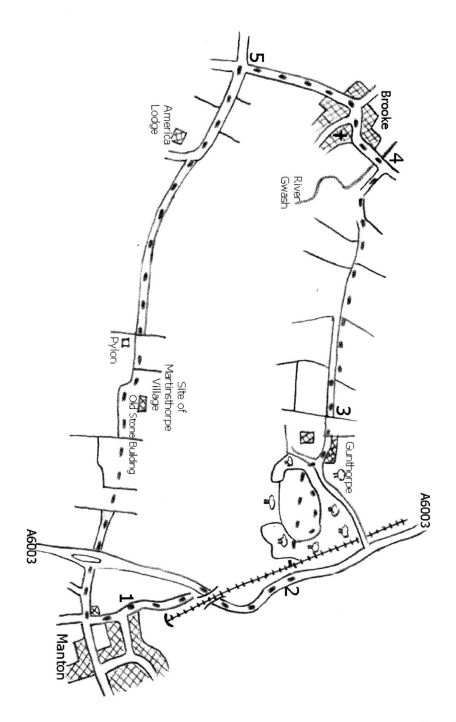

5   Cuckoo Spinney

$7^1/_2$ Miles $3^1/_2$ Hours

Park in the Whitwell car park off the A606 west of Whitwell village, on the north shore of Rutland Water. Pay and display; toilets, café and shop on site.

1   Walk back to the A606 via the path next to the entrance road, turn right at the brown cycle/byway sign past the church. Turn right at the road into the village and then left at the signpost by the 'Noel Arms' entrance. Go across the patio; turn left up the steps on the left, past the climbing frame and left over the stile in the corner.

2   Bear right around the hedge corner and continue over two more stiles. Keep direction along field edge and cross the boundary at the marker post. Turn left at the next boundary, walk 50yds to a marker post and turn right along the edge of the field with the hedge to the right. Go over two sleeper footbridges at the boundaries; continue to the hedge corner and turn right. Turn left at the corner and go up to the road. Walk over the green triangle and along the road ahead towards Exton, just past the '30' signs turn right over the stile.

3   Walk down the bridleway and turn right over the stile next to the double gate. Cross this field parallel to the fence on the right and cross the next stile. Continue ahead along the obvious path that turns to the right and crosses the stream. Go over the stile, turn right then left through the end of Cuckoo Spinney, cross another stile and follow the path at the foot of the slope. Turn left over the footbridge at the top of this shallow valley; walk up the slope and over the stile at the top. Turn right at the fence corner on the right and follow the edge of the field with the fence on the right past the garden to a stile/footbridge. Cross; turn left and walk diagonally up the slope to the stile almost hidden 50yds from the corner. Turn left and around the edge of the field to the sign at the side of the road.

4   Turn left along the road, go around a right hand corner and take the path signposted across the stile to the right as the road starts to turn left again. Walk a right angles away from the road, over the hump in the middle of the field to the sti in the left hand side of the wood, Horn Mill Spinney, ahead. Cross this narrow spinney on the obvious path and then walk diagonally right over the next field. Th field may be under cultivation but the track should be visible, the path leads to a yellow-topped post just to the right of a telegraph pole. Carry on along the farm

To Oakham

Whitwell Car Park

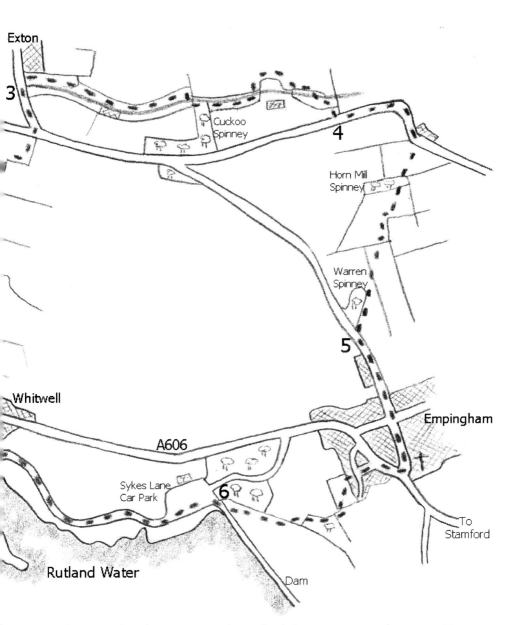

track ahead, turn right; then cross a stile to the left, next to a marker post. Turn diagonally right, the yellow top of the next marker post can be seen against the dark background of the wood. The path should be clear through any crops in this field. Go over the stile and maintain direction along the left hand side of the wood (Warren Spinney) to the road.

Completed on the next Page (Fourteen)

6:H

Completion of Cuckoo Spinney walk from Page Thirteen

5   Turn left and walk downhill into Empingham, go straight across at the crossroads into Church Street. Go past the church to the A606 and turn right (Audit Hall Road). Take the left turn into Nook Lane past the sign saying 'No access to Rutland Water', go straight on at the T-junction down the grass path between houses. Cross the stile, turn half left and cross the field diagonally to the corner of the wood (the marker post is visible above the stile). Go over this stile, turn right to the next, step over this and walk through the wood on the obvious path. Keep direction over the stile at the end of the wood, the field and a final stile near to a trig point. Turn right and continue alongside the fence, as this ends turn left to the gate at the end of the dam and turn right through it.

6   Join the tarmac path going anti-clockwise around Rutland Water, past Sykes Lane car park and facilities, keep to the hardcore and tarmac path closest to the waters edge around Whitwell Creek, to the Whitwell car park and your vehicle.

---

6   Fort Henry Lake

$4^1/_2$ Miles $1^3/_4$ Hours

An easy walk, mainly on tarmac bridleways with little traffic; open and bleak in winter. Park in Exton village. No toilets.

1   Start from the green triangle at the junction of New Field Road, where Stamford road becomes Top Street. Walk along Top Street and turn right into West End, go left over the cattle grid and then right past the poplar trees. Cross the next cattle grid and continue past the wood.

2   Bear right at the end of the wood at the junction with another bridleway. Carry on along this bridleway with the Tunneley Wood to the right and bear right again at the next junction. Keep going on this hardcore then tarmac road for a fraction over a mile past trees and into the dip by Fort Henry Lake.

3   Turn right at the footpath sign as the road starts to rise again, cross the stile and go down the field and through the gate to the bottom of Lower Lake.

4   Go right, along the bottom of lower Lake, cross the stile and continue on the road up the slope. Bear left at the junction, continuing uphill, past the rail barrier over the cattle grid and down the tree lined avenue into Exton and your vehicle.

6:H

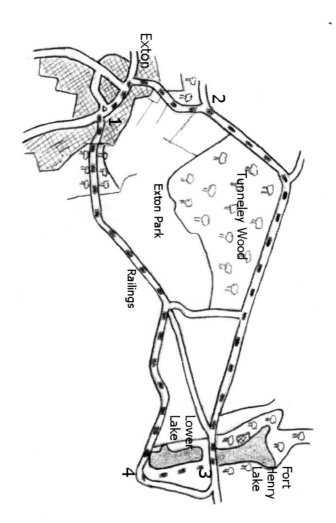

Fort Henry was built between 1786-89, named after Henry Noel, 6th Earl of Gainsborough. It was used as a family base for boating activities on the lake, including re-enactments of Famous naval battles. The two lakes were created during the early 18th century, originally with some miniature waterfalls at the end of Lower Lake.

The Noel family have owned the Exton estate since the early 17th century; Edward Noel became Earl of Gainsborough in 1682. The title became extinct in 1798 but was recreated for the family in 1841. The present Hall dates from 1850 when the existing building was greatly increased in size.

7   Braunston-in-Rutland

6 Miles   3 Hours

Park in Braunston village, no toilets, two local pubs.

1 Start from the church; turn right down Wood Lane, cross the river and walk uphill for nearly half a mile. As the road turns sharp left, carry straight on along the bridleway past the signpost; the tarmac surface soon becomes a stone topped narrower track. Keep left as a route branches off to a gate and go through a gap next to a metal gate; follow the wide track ahead between trees. Maintain direction on the left hand field edge bearing right to a marker post at a gate.

2 Go through and turn right along the wide, grassy, hedged track; continue through a metal gate, follow the track left and go through the narrow wooden gate on the right.

3 Follow the track ahead, left of the narrow wooden gate on the right and keep direction to a double metal gate at a signpost. Go through the first gate and turn right, downslope between hedges, to the gate at the road. Pass through and turn immediate left over the stile.

4 Keep ahead over the field and the stile marked by a yellow top post. Keep direction through the gate to the road and turn right, up to the T-Junction.

5 Cross this road, go through the gate opposite and down the left hand side of the field. Be careful on this next section to the river there are a lot of gates and the paths may be confusing; the way is reasonably well marked and the direction easily kept. Continue through the gate on the left and bear right, uphill, through the next gate at a yellow top marker post. Maintain direction along the field edge and through two more gates. Cross a narrow field end and go through two more gates, to the yellow topped post at the bottom left. Follow the next field's left hand edge into a dip and up again to the corner, through the gateway into the left hand field.

6 Continue down the right hand side of this field, through the gate and downhill across the field. Step over the River Gwash; go through the gate and uphill along the enclosed bridleway. Go through the gate at the top and cross the road.

7 Bear slight right through the narrow gate to the top right hand corner of this field, through this narrow gate and along the left hand side of the field, through the next gate and then cross the field to the gate towards the centre of the hedge ahead. Keep direction between hedges all the way to the marker post.

8 Turn immediately right through a gateway with no gate and go down the right hand field edge, through a gate and bear right, through the marked gate. Follow this narrow hedged path downslope, turning left to the road in Braunston village to find your vehicle.

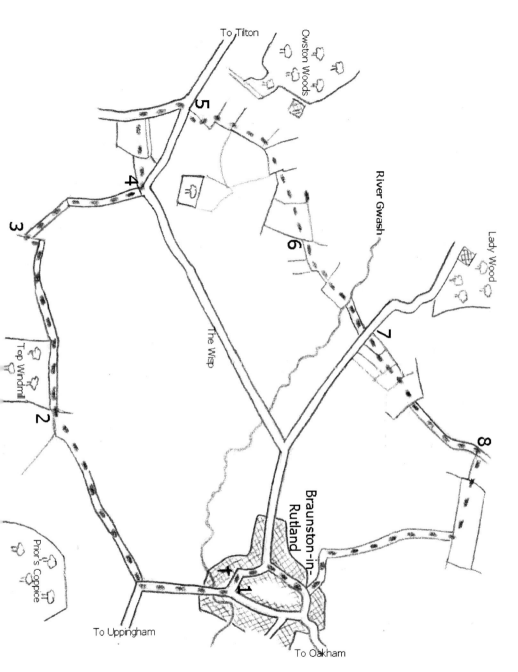

To Tilton

Owston Woods

5

4

3

River Gwash

6

Lady Wood

The Wisp

Tap Windmill

2

7

8

Braunston-in-
Rutland

Prior's Coppice

To Uppingham

To Oakham

:H

8 Prior's Coppice

$4^1/_2$ Miles   2 Hours

Find a parking space in Braunston village; no toilets, two local pubs.

1 Start from the junction close to the church; take the road towards Leighfield and
Ridlington. Bear left past the signpost, over the footbridge and carry on left
between houses and up the grass path with the stone wall to the right.

2 Go over the stile and up the left hand field edge. Cross the footbridge/stile at
the top and continue direction with the fence to the right; through the gate and on
to the next boundary. Step over this stile and bear slight left with the trees to the
left, to the yellow top marker post.

3 Follow the field edge right and go past the next marker post to the enclosed
path at the end, turn right, between hedges and trees and carry on along the left
hand field edge through the boundary to the road. Turn left to the signpost on the
left for Leighfield Lodge.

4 Take this tarmac driveway to the right for a mile and a quarter to the junction
and turn right for 150yds to the marker post on the right.

5 Step over the stile next to the gate, cross the field, upslope to the opposite
corner. Go over the stile here and turn right, through the stony gap. Keep direction
up the field edge with the hedge to the left.

6 At the top, cross the estate road and carry on with Prior's Coppice to the right.
As the trees end, keep ahead across the field and the stile at the far side; continue
direction over the stile in the narrow end.

7 Bear right along the farm track to the road. Walk up the road back to
Braunston and your vehicle.

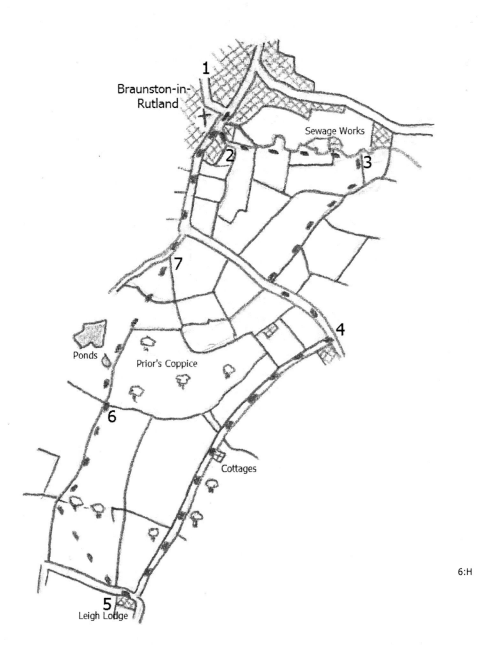

Braunston-in-Rutland

Sewage Works

Ponds

Prior's Coppice

Cottages

Leigh Lodge

6:H

9 Shacklewell

$6^1/_4$ Miles 3 Hours

Park in Empingham village, no toilets, local shop, pub the 'White Horse'. Muddy in wet weather, best in summer when the ground is hard

1 Start from the church, turn left along the A606 (actually straight on!) cross the bridge over the River Gwash and turn left over the stile just past the woodland. Keep direction over the next stile with the wood to the left and cross another stile. Maintain direction first with the hedge on the right then over the open field. Cross the stile ahead and keep direction over the field beyond, which may be under cultivation but the track should be visible (look for the yellow topped posts). Go over the stile and the field beyond to the stile in the top right hand corner.

2 After this double stile cross the field diagonally right to the tree on the far side, the path should be visible through any crop. Continue direction over the next field, behind Shacklewell Farm to stiles each side of a farm track and cross the next field, which again may be under cultivation, to the right of the stand of trees. Continue past the trees and across the next narrow field to the rear of Shacklewell Cottage. The path now takes a shallow diagonal right almost parallel with the road, before reaching it in the next dip.

3 Cross and turn left, along the verge. Almost at the top of the rise take the footpath signposted right, the path should be visible through any crops, to the bridleway on the other side of the hedge.

The path from here to point 5 was re-aligned a few years ago, the route and the map may differ from that shown on the Ordnance Survey map.

4 Turn right here, down to the narrow belt of trees and bear left. Follow this path with the trees to the right for a fraction under a mile to a gate just after the trees end.

5 Go through the gate; turn left and go on a shallow diagonal away from the hedge to a small gate marked by a yellow top post. Follow the path right, along the edge of the field; cross the stile and turn slight right after the next stile at the corner of New Wood. Walk past the end of the trees close to the mast ahead and keep direction to the road.

Instructions completed on next Page (Twenty Two)

6:

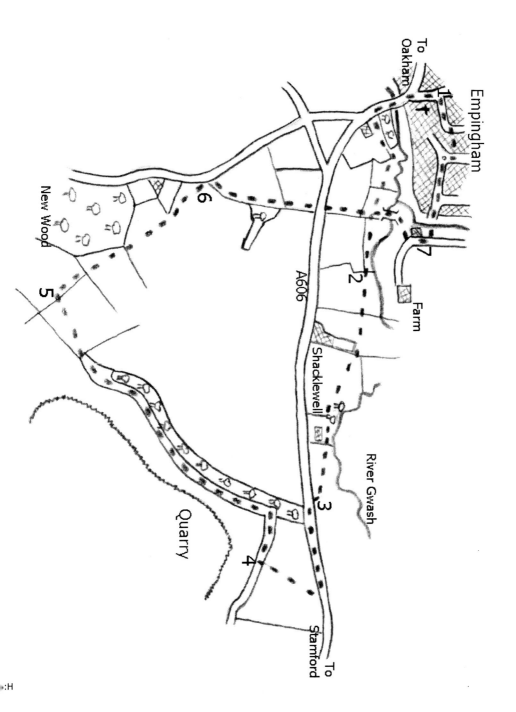

<u>Completion of Shacklewell walk from Page Twenty</u>

6   Turn right immediately, signposted Hereward Way, through the gate and down the right hand side of the field with the hedge to the right. Continue to the road, cross and maintain direction down slope over the track of the outward journey. Go over the iron footbridge across the Gwash and turn right to the road at the end of the cottage. Take the road to the left over the cattle grid to a signpost pointing left

7   Cross the stile and a narrow field; go over the footbridge and continue direction over the field and along Willoughby Drive ahead. Turn right at the green circle, left through the kissing Gate and walk ahead down Crocket Lane to the Church.

---

10   Langham

5 Miles   2$^1/_4$ Hours

Find a parking space in Langham village. No toilets. Pubs the 'Wheatsheaf' and the 'Noel Arms'.

1   Start from the junction of the A606 with Burley Road; walk away from the A606 through the village towards Burley and Cottesmore. As the road bears right, go straight on up the narrow tarmac road past the footpath signpost. Continue through the kissing gate along the wide hedged path, keep direction past the farm buildings and houses and turn left over a stile.

2   Cross the field on a diagonal to the far corner, step over the stile at the yellow top post and bear left through the trees. Go over the bridge and continue ahead on the farm track up the left hand field edge; follow the track right at the marker post. Bear right; turn left at a marker disc on a gatepost and right at the marker post in the corner.

3   At the stile by the metal gate turn left between the fence and the hedge, the track bears left past a small wood to the road. Turn right and immediate left at the signpost in the corner.

4   After the first double bend keep direction along this bridleway for three quarters of a mile, past the aerial and through the wide gateway next to a marker post. Carry on along the left hand field edge, bear left in the next corner keeping on the left hand side of the field; go through the boundary up to the stile on the left.

5   Cross and walk downhill on the grass track between fields with the dyke to the left, bear slight right and keep straight on over the footbridge past the marker post with a hedge now left. Turn right at the signpost in the corner and go up to the

6:

marker post cross the footbridge left and turn right back to the original direction the
edge now to the right. Continue to the corner.

● Turn left along the field edge and keep direction through the narrow gap next to

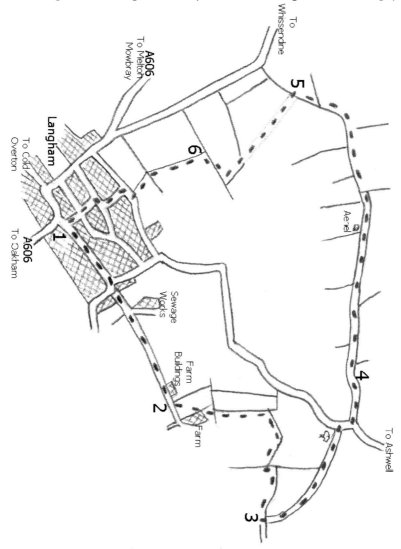

he marker post, turn right and follow the track around the edge of the field over
he stile and onto the road. Turn right and immediate left down Orchard Road, at
he end turn right and immediate left into Bridge Street. Carry on past the 'Noel
rms', this leads to the start point at the junction of the A606 and Burley Road.

The 'Walking Close to' Series

South and South West

The New Forest (North and West)
Romsey and the Test Valley
Cheddar Gorge
Exmouth and East Devon
Corsham and Box (Wiltshire)
The Quantock Hills (West Somerset)
Blandford Forum (Dorset)

The New Forest (South and East)
The East Devon Coast
Glastonbury and the City of Wells
The Avon near Bath
The Avon near Chippenham (Wiltshire)
Shaftesbury (Dorset)
Bradford-on-Avon (Wiltshire)

East Anglia and Lincolnshire

The Nene near Peterborough
Lavenham (Suffolk)
The Nene Valley Railway near Wansford
The Nene near Oundle
The Great North Road near Stilton
Bury St Edmunds
Norfolk Broads (Northern Area)
Southwold and the Suffolk Coast
North West Norfolk (Hunstanton and Wells)
North Norfolk (Cromer and Sheringham)
The Lincolnshire Wolds (North)
The Stour near Sudbury (Suffolk)
Chelmsford
Epping Forest (Essex/North London)
The Colne near Colchester
Thetford Forest (Norfolk/Suffolk)
The Great Ouse in Huntingdonshire
The Torpel Way (Stamford to Peterborough)

Grafham Water (Huntingdonshire)
Dedham Vale (Suffolk/Essex)
The Cam and the Granta near Cambridge
Lincoln
The Welland near Stamford
The Isle of Ely
Norfolk Broads (Southern Area)
Aldeburgh, Snape and Thorpeness
Clare, Cavendish and Haverhill
Bourne and the Deepings
The Lincolnshire Wolds (South)
The Orwell near Ipswich
Stowmarket (Suffolk)
Hertford and the Lee Valley
Newmarket
The Great Ouse near King's Lynn
South Lincolnshire

Midlands

The Nene near Thrapston
The Nene near Wellingborough
The River Ise near Kettering
The Nene near Northampton
Rockingham Forest (Northamptonshire)
Daventry and North West Northamptonshire
Rugby
Stratford-upon-Avon
Rutland Water
Eye Brook near Uppingham
The Soar near Leicester
Lutterworth (Leicestershire)
The Vale of Belvoir (North Leicestershire)
Melton Mowbray
The Welland near Market Harborough
Banbury
South West Herefordshire

The Great Ouse near Bedford
Woburn Abbey (Bedfordshire)
Sherwood Forest
Pitsford Water (Northamptonshire)
The Thames near Oxford
The Trent near Nottingham
The Vale of White Horse
Henley-on-Thames
The River Pang (Reading/Newbury)
The Great Ouse north of Milton Keynes
The Cotswolds near Witney
The Malvern Hills
The Dukeries (Sherwood Forest)
The Severn near Worcester
Woodstock and Blenheim Palace
The Kennet near Newbury

Cumbria

Cartmel and Southern Lakeland

Cheshire

Chester and Delamere Forest (2015)

6:H